# A Little Mexican Cookbook

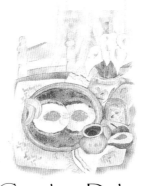

## Carolyn Dehnel

**ILLUSTRATED BY MARIAN CLARK DE MONREAL**

## Appletree Press

First published in 1991 by
The Appletree Press Ltd, 7 James Street South,
Belfast BT2 8DL.
Copyright © 1991 The Appletree Press, Ltd. Illustrations ©
1991 Marian Clark de Monreal used under Exclusive License to
The Appletree Press, Ltd.
Printed in Hong Kong. All rights reserved.

British Library Cataloguing in Publication Data
Dehnel, Carolyn
A Little Mexican Cookbook
I. Food, Mexican dishes. Recipes
I. Title
641.5972

ISBN: 0-86281-273-9


First published in the United States in 1991
by Chronicle Books, 275 Fifth Street,
San Francisco, CA 94103

ISBN 0-87701-860-X

9 8 7 6 5 4 3 2 1

# Introduction

Mexican cuisine is a rich *mélange* of several different cultures. While it rests on Aztec and Mayan foundations, the influence of Spanish cooking since the Conquest has refined and changed it. This gives Mexican dishes an unexpected subtlety of flavour – especially to those who think Chilli con Carne typically Mexican – which it isn't. The subtlety comes not only from a combination of different cultures but also from the combination and balance of different chillis, nuts, seeds and spices. This book seeks to introduce only a few of the jewels of the Mexican kitchen; you will find some surprises from the rich Mole Poblana con Pavo to the simple but flavourful Pozole. The aromas and tastes of Mexican food should be easily achieved as most ingredients are available from the supermarket, delicatessen, or ethnic shop. A note about chillis – tinned jalapeño pepper (very hot) and green chillis (cool) are readily available in most good supermarkets or ethnic markets. Also available are a variety of African and Caribbean chillis – experiment with combinations of these to arrive at a taste you prefer. Some recipes in this book do list the traditional chillis which may not be available. Experiment! After all, there are more than ninety-four kinds cultivated in Mexico. Mexican cheese is white, mild and slightly salty; to substitute, use Lancashire, Wensleydale or Cheshire. Do use absolutely fresh ingredients – this is one of the hallmarks of the Mexican kitchen.

## A note on measures

Metric, imperial and volume measurements have been given for all the recipes. For perfect results use one set only. Metric measures should be used where no American measure is shown, as for meat weights. Spoon measurements are level except where otherwise indicated. Seasonings can of course be adjusted according to taste. Recipes are for four.

# Chocolate Mexicana

## *Chocolate Drink*

Chocolate was the royal drink in pre-Columbian Mexico. Early in the morning, in cafés all over Mexico, this drink is served with sweet breads of all kinds, and with *churros* – strips of dough, deep-fried and coated in sugar. In Mexico it is possible to buy thick discs of chocolate already mixed with sugar, spices, and almonds for melting to make this warming drink. This recipe produces the next best taste. While it can be made at any time in the day, it is a wonderful breakfast drink. Serve with cinnamon sticks as stirrers.

| | |
|---|---|
| 1½ oz/50 g unsweetened chocolate | ½ tsp vanilla essence |
| ¾ pt/450 ml/2 cups milk | 2 tbsp dark brown sugar |
| ¼ tsp ground cinnamon | 2 cinnamon sticks |

serves 2

Gently melt the chocolate. Warm the milk and stir in the remaining ingredients. Add to the melted chocolate. Froth in a blender or with a *molinillo,* a wooden whisk twirled between your palms especially made for creating a froth on liquids.

# Café de Olla

## *Coffee with Cinnamon*

Traditionally made and served in handleless earthenware pots, this drink can also be made in a saucepan.

| | |
|---|---|
| 4 cups water | 2-in piece of stick cinnamon |
| 4 ozs/½ cup dark brown sugar | 4 whole cloves |

*4 tbsp regular-grind dark-roasted coffee*

Heat the water, sugar, cinnamon and cloves in a saucepan, stirring until sugar is dissolved. Add the coffee, bring to the boil, and simmer for a minute or two. Stir, cover and leave for the grounds to settle before serving.

# Huevos Rancheros
## *Ranch-style Eggs*

Ranch-style eggs make a dish that is delicious any time of the day from morning to midnight. It is especially good for breakfast with plenty of extra tortillas.

*4 corn tortillas (see p 28)*
*2 fl oz/50 ml/¼ cup corn oil*
*Salsa Caliente (see p 11), warm*
*Frijoles Refritos (see p 31), warm*
*4 large eggs, fried*
*8 oz/225 g/1 cup white cheese, grated*
*1 avocado, sliced*

Cook tortillas in corn oil and keep warm. Spread sauce on four large plates, then layer tortillas with beans, fried eggs and grated cheese. Garnish each plate with sliced avocado. Serve with extra sauce and cheese.

# Huevos Oaxacqueños

## *Oaxaca Eggs*

Oaxaca state was one of the centres of pre-Conquest Indian cultures and its cuisine remains Indian in influence. Oaxaca City is the centre for those interested in visiting the temple cities of Monte Alban and Mitla.

---

Salsa Caliente *(see p 11)*
*4-8 eggs*
*tortillas (see p 28)*
*lime quarters*
*bunch fresh coriander, chopped*
*4 oz/125 g/1 cup white cheese, grated*

---

Warm the sauce in a shallow pan. As it begins to bubble, break the eggs into the sauce. Cover and poach to the desire consistency. Serve with tortillas, lime quarters, fresh coriander, and grated cheese. For a large crowd, scramble the desired number of eggs and stir in the warm sauce. Serve with lots of tortillas.

# Salsa Caliente

## *Hot Sauce*

Cooked sauces are served as accompaniments to all types of dishes – meat, fish and vegetable. They can be as *caliente* (hot) as you wish by adjusting the number of peppers you use. This sauce is often used as a dip for tortillas.

| | |
|---|---|
| 4 large tomatoes, grilled, peeled, seeded and chopped | small onion, finely chopped |
| 1-3 jalapeño peppers | 2 tbsp corn oil |
| clove garlic, crushed | chicken stock |
| | salt |

Combine the grilled tomatoes with peppers and garlic and blend to a purée. Cook onion in oil until opaque. Add tomato mixture and cook 15-20 minutes or until no longer 'raw' tasting. The mixture should be smooth; add chicken stock if too thick. Season with salt to taste. This sauce freezes well.

# Salsa Cruda

## *Uncooked Sauce*

A bowl of uncooked *salsa* is usually found on the table at any meal. Should you have any left over, fry a little chopped onion, add to the sauce and cook for future use.

---

*2 large tomatoes, peeled, seeded and chopped*
*bunch spring onions, thinly sliced*
*1-3 jalapeño peppers*
*bunch fresh coriander, chopped*
*2 tbsp tomato juice or cold water*
*salt to taste*

---

Combine all the ingredients in a small bowl and set aside to marinade for at least an hour before serving.

# Guacamole

## *Avocado Sauce*

This versatile dish can be used as a sauce, dip, or salad.

---

*1 large ripe avocado*
*1 small tomato, peeled, seeded and chopped*
*¼ small onion, finely chopped*
*1 or more canned green chilli*
*sprigs of coriander*
*salt and pepper*

---

Peel and mash avocado flesh. Mix with all other ingredients and pile into a serving dish. If you are not serving immediately, cover the dish with foil or plastic wrap and refrigerate. Serve as a dip with taco chips or fried tortilla triangles.

# Sopa de Frijoles Negros

## *Black Bean Soup*

Black beans make an interesting taste variation in this soup. You can use leftover Frijoles de Olla (see p 31) if black beans aren't available.

| | |
|---|---|
| *12 oz/350 g/2 cups black beans* | *salt to taste* |
| *large onion, finely chopped* | *bunch radishes, thinly sliced* |
| *3 cloves garlic, crushed* | *4 green chillis, chopped* |
| *meaty pork bone* | *¼ pt/150 ml/½ cup soured cream* |
| *1 tsp oregano* | *lime wedges* |
| *2 tbsp tomato purée* | |

Soak beans in water overnight. Rinse and put into large pot and cover with water. Bring to the boil and boil for 5 minutes. Remove from heat, pour off water and rinse beans. Cover beans with cold water and bring back to boil. Cook until done (approx 30-45 mins) then add onion, garlic, pork bone and oregano. Cook 1½-2 hours more or until beans are very soft. Add tomato purée and salt to taste. Serve with remaining ingredients as garnishes.

# Sopa de Cerveza

## *Beer Soup*

Beer was brewed in Mexico before the Conquest. Modern beers are German-style *bach* beer.

*16 boiling onions, peeled*
*2 fl oz/50 ml/¼ cup corn oil*
*2½ pts/1½ ltrs/5 cups well-seasoned chicken stock*

$\frac{1}{4}$ pt/150 ml/$\frac{2}{3}$ cup lager
4 oz/125 g/1 cup white cheese, grated

Fry onions in oil for 10 minutes. Add stock and beer and simmer for 20 more minutes. Serve hot with the cheese sprinkled over.

# Sopa de Albóndigas

## Meat-ball Soup

Albóndigas are meat-balls. They can be formed to any size from golf-ball to walnut (when they become Albóndiguitas – little meat-balls). For this soup they should be Albóndiguitas.

| | |
|---|---|
| 1 lb/450 g minced beef | 1 tsp salt |
| small onion, finely chopped | $\frac{1}{2}$ tsp dried thyme |
| 1$\frac{1}{2}$ oz/50 g/1 cup soft breadcrumbs | $\frac{1}{4}$ tsp ground nutmeg |
| | bay leaf |
| 1 canned chipotle chilli (if you can find them) | 3$\frac{1}{2}$ pts/2 qts/7 cups beef broth or consommé |
| 1 egg, slightly beaten | 4 serrano chillis, chopped |
| 5-6 tbsp milk | lime wedges |
| 2 tbsp chopped fresh coriander | |

Mix beef, onion, breadcrumbs and chilli (if used). In a separate bowl mix egg, milk, coriander, salt, thyme and nutmeg; add to meat and mix well. Make bite-sized meat-balls and drop with bay leaf into simmering broth. Cover and cook 45-60 minutes. Serve with chillis and lime wedges as garnish.

# Arroz Blanco

## *White Rice*

This is a *sopa seca* (dry soup), which is a course in itself and which is usually made from rice or pasta.

***

2 fl oz/50 ml/¼ cup corn oil
medium onion, finely chopped
clove garlic, crushed
8 oz/225 g/1 cup rice
¾ pt/450 ml/2 cups well-seasoned chicken stock
2 oz/60 g/½ cup green peas
1 carrot, diced and blanched
green chilli, chopped

***

Fry onion and garlic in a heavy-based pan until the onion is transluscent. Add the rice and fry for 5 minutes. Add the stock and bring to a boil. Cover the pan, reduce the heat and cook for 15-20 minutes or until all the stock is absorbed. Add the green peas, carrot and chilli and mix well. Cover and allow the added vegetables to warm through.

**Arroz Rojo** When cooking the onion and garlic, add 2 medium peeled and chopped tomatoes, 2 tbsp tomato purée, and substitute one-quarter of the stock with tomato juice. Continue as directed, omitting the peas and carrot.

**Arroz Verde** Before cooking, purée onion and garlic with a bunch of fresh coriander. Cook in oil and proceed as before, adding chilli at end of cooking time. Garnish with slices of lime or avocado.

# Picadillo

## Minced Meat Stew

This spicy meat stew can be used in many Mexican dishes – for example, as a filling for tortilla-based dishes such as Tacos and Enchiladas, in Tamales, or Chiles en Nogada. The list is infinite.

1 oz/30 g/2 tbsp cooking oil
medium onion, finely chopped
2 cloves garlic, crushed
1½ lb/675 g pork or beef, finely chopped or coarsely minced
1 lb/450 g large tomatoes, peeled, seeded and chopped
2 tbsp tomato purée
3 oz/100 g/½ cup raisins (optional)
2 tbsp red wine vinegar
1 tbsp chilli powder
1 tsp ground cinnamon
1 tsp ground cumin
1 tsp ground coriander
½ tsp ground cloves
1-3 jalapeño pepper
salt and pepper
¼ cup slivered almonds (optional)

Heat oil and brown onion and garlic; add meat and brown. Add next 9 ingredients. Cover and cook slowly for 30 minutes. If the mixture dries out, add a little water. When cooked, add the peppers and salt and pepper to taste. If used, fry the almonds in a little oil and sprinkle over the Picadillo. The mixture should be dry. This freezes well.

# Tamales

## *Corn Dumplings*

These corn dumplings were being eaten by the Aztecs at the time of the Conquest. A basic food, they can be filled with most anything – meat, fish, vegetable or any of the sauces. You must use *masa harina* – ordinary corn meal will not do. This recipe makes 30 dumplings.

---

*60 dried corn husks or 30 squares foil lined with oiled greaseproof paper (approx. 8 in/20 cm sq)*
*8 oz/225 g/1 cup lard*
*1½ lb/675 g/5 cups masa harina*
*2 tbsp baking powder*
*1 tsp salt*
*¾ pt/450 ml/2 cups chicken stock*
*4 cups Picadillo (see p 20)*

---

The night before, cover the corn husks, if available, with boiling water and soak. Before starting, drain the husks and dry well. Beat the lard until creamy. Combine the flour with the baking powder and salt and gradually add to the lard until it is all used. Add the stock until the dough is pliable but not too wet. Place two husks on a flat surface. Spread with the dough to a depth of ⅛ in/½ cm. Leave about 1 in/2½ cm all the way around free of dough. Spoon 2 tbsp of filling down the center. Roll the corn husks so the dough meets and makes a package with the meat visible at both ends. Fold husks over one end and place in steamer open end up. Use the same method for foil squares. Continue until all dough and filling are used. Cover and steam for 1½ hours. These dumplings can be frozen; allow to defrost and steam for a further half hour.

# Pozole

## *Meat Stew with Corn*

Pozole is said to be the perfect 'pick you up' at the end of a night on the town. Hominy is a specially treated corn and should be used if available.

*1 lb/450 g pork, in small cubes*
*1 lb/450 g beef, in small cubes*
*4 chicken legs*
*2 tbsp corn oil*
*medium onion, finely chopped*
*2 cloves garlic, crushed*
*3½ pts/2 ltrs/7 cups beef stock*
*8 oz/225 g /2 cups hominy or corn*
*1-3 tbsp chilli powder*
*bunch spring onions, chopped*
*bunch fresh coriander, chopped*
*bunch radishes, sliced*

Brown meats and chicken in oil. Add onion and garlic and cook until light golden. Add stock and cook until the meat is tender. Add the hominy or corn and chilli powder to taste and cook a further 45 minutes. Serve with hot tortillas and garnish with spring onions, fresh coriander and radishes.

# Mancha Manteles de Pollo y Cerdo

## Chicken and Pork Tablecloth Stainer

Mancha Manteles literally means tablecloth stainer – a warning to those enjoying this dish. It is traditionally served on Corpus Christi Day.

---

1 lb/450 g lean pork
4 chicken breasts
½ oz/15 g/1 tbsp cooking oil
1 oz/30 g/24 whole blanched almonds
1 cinnamon stick
1 tbsp sesame seed
4 ancho chillis
1 tbsp cider vinegar
2 large tomatoes, grilled, peeled and seeded
4 slices pineapple, in chunks
2 tart or cooking apples, quartered
plantain or banana, in chunks
salt and pepper

---

Cover the pork with water, bring to the boil and skim. Cover and simmer for 25 minutes. Remove pork from water and cool. Reserve broth. Brown the chicken in the oil, and remove. Separately brown the almonds, cinnamon stick, sesame seed and chillis. Blend in a blender or food processor with the vinegar, tomatoes and a little of the pork broth to make a sauce. Cook fruit in the oil for 5 minutes. Add sauce to pan. Return chicken and pork to pan. Add enough broth to make a thickish sauce and season. Cover and cook slowly for an additional half hour.

# Tortillas

No need to translate 'tortilla', the basic bread of Mexico that can be fried flat, filled and rolled, or fried into cup or boat shapes ready for filling. While available to buy ready-made, they taste better if made from scratch. The knack for making them round comes with practice. Below are two recipes – one made with *masa harina*, a specially treated corn meal. Plain corn meal will not work. The second, made with plain flour, is typical of northern Mexico. Both can be made snack size and eaten plain or filled.

## Tortillas de Maiz (Corn Tortillas)

| |
|---|
| 10½ oz/275 g/2 cups masa harina |
| 9 fl oz/250 ml/1 cup + 2 tbs warm water |

Combine the two ingredients to make a pliable dough. Divide it into balls of desired size and roll between two pieces of cling film into circles and then cook each circle on both sides on a hot griddle

## Tortillas de Harina (Flour Tortillas)

| | |
|---|---|
| 8 oz/225 g/2 cups plain flour | 3 oz/100 g/6 tbsp lard |
| 2 tsp salt | 3 fl oz/100 ml/6 tbsp warm |
| ½ tsp bicarbonate of soda | water |

Sieve together the flour, salt and bicarbonate of soda in a bowl. Cut the lard into cubes and work into the flour as for pastry. Add water and make a dough. Knead for 5 minutes, adding flour if too wet. Divide into 12 balls and roll into very thin circles on a floured surface. Cook both sides lightly on a hot griddle.

**Enchiladas** Roll lightly cooked tortillas around any filling – meat, cheese, Picadillo, or Salsa with soured cream. Put into baking dish,

# A Little Mexican Cookbook

## Carolyn Dehnel

ILLUSTRATED BY MARIAN CLARK DE MONREAL

### Guacamole
#### Avocado Sauce

This versatile dish can be used as a sauce, dip, or salad.

1 large ripe avocado
1 small tomato, peeled, seeded and chopped
½ small onion, finely chopped
1 or more canned green chilli
sprigs of coriander
salt and pepper

Peel and mash avocado flesh. Mix with all other ingredients into a serving dish. If you are not serving immediately, dish with foil or plastic wrap and refrigerate. Serve as a taco chips or fried tortilla triangles.

Appletree Press

cover with Salsa Caliente and/or cheese and heat in oven until cheese melts.

**Tacos** Serve lightly cooked tortillas with different fillings on the side so guests may help themselves.

**Tostados** These are tortillas that have been fried until golden brown and crisp, then covered with combinations of cooked meats, poultry, fish, sauces, chillis, etc.

# Frijoles de Olla

## *Beans*

A pot of beans is kept on the back burner in most Mexican kitchens. Beans are served not only at lunch or dinner but also at breakfast.

| | |
|---|---|
| 12 oz/350 g/2 cups pinto, black, or red kidney beans | 2 cloves garlic, crushed |
| | 3-5 tbsp chili powder |
| medium onion, finely chopped | salt |

Soak the beans in water overnight. Drain, rinse and cover with water in a large pot. Bring to the boil and cook for 5 minutes. Drain, rinse and cover again with cold water. Add onion, garlic, and chili powder. Cook until beans are ready. Add salt to taste.

### Frijoles Refritos (Refried Beans)
The traditional way to serve beans. Drain the cooked beans and reserve the liquid. In a large pan fry a finely chopped onion in lard. Add the beans and mash them to a rough pulp. Continue to fry, adding about 6 tbsp of lard, grated cheese and bean liquid in small quantities until flavoured to taste and the beans are a creamy dry paste. Sprinkle with grated cheese and serve.

# Mole Poblana con Pavo

## *Puebla-style Sauce with Turkey*

The sauce for Mole Poblana con Pavo is the classic in the Mexican kitchen. Its versatility is demonstrable. It can be served over fish, meat and poultry and used in Enchiladas, Tacos or Tamales.

| | |
|---|---|
| mixture of chillis available (about 3) | 1¼ oz/40 g/3 tbsp pumpkin seed, toasted |
| 2½ oz/70 g/⅓ cup lard | 2½ oz/70 g/½ cup almonds, toasted |
| 2 oz/60 g/½ cup sesame seed, toasted | 1½ oz/50 g/¼ cup raw peanuts, toasted |
| ¼ tsp coriander seed, toasted | 1 stale corn tortilla |
| 10 peppercorns | ¾ pt/450 ml/2 cups chicken broth |
| 4 whole cloves | 2 oz/60 g unsweetened chocolate |
| 6 small green or red tomatoes, peeled and seeded | salt |
| large onion, chopped | |
| 1½ oz/50 g/¼ cup raisins | |
| 1½ lb/675 g cooked turkey | |

Fry chillis in lard and make a purée. Use whatever chillis are available – dried, fresh, tinned, or a combination. You want enough to have at least ¼ pt/150 ml/½ cup chilli purée. Return purée to pan and cook for 10 minutes. Grind the sesame and coriander seed, peppercorns and cloves together. Add tomatoes and onion and continue to blend. Add remaining ingredients and blend until very smooth. As the mixture will be warm, the chocolate should melt as it is ground. To make a smoother sauce, put through a processor or blender. Cook 30 minutes. If the sauce is too thick, add more chicken stock. The sauce is best made ahead. Serve over warm poached or roast turkey, with Guacamole (see p 00), beans and rice. The sauce can be frozen.

# Pollo Pibil

*Barbecued Chicken*

A *pibil* is a Yucatecan pit barbecue. Traditionally, this dish is first wrapped in banana leaves and then buried in coals in the *pibil* for slow cooking. Unless you have a banana tree handy, use pieces of greaseproof or foil.

---

2 tbsp tandoori mix or anchiote paste
1/4 tsp whole cumin seed
1/4 tsp dried oregano
4 cloves garlic, crushed
2 fl oz/50 ml/1/4 cup tart orange juice
dash Tabasco
freshly ground black pepper
4 chicken quarters
medium onion, thinly sliced
2 fl oz/50 ml/1/4 cup corn oil
2 large tomatoes, peeled and sliced
4 squares double greaseproof paper or foil

---

Prepare a marinade by combining one half of tandoori mix or paste and next six ingredients. Dry chicken and cover in marinade; leave overnight in a cool place. Cook onion in oil until soft with remaining tandoori mix. Remove onion and sauté tomato slices. Distribute onion and tomatoes among greaseproof paper squares. Place chicken quarters on top, meaty side down. Fold paper to make secure packages and place in oven pan. Cook for half an hour in a pre-heated oven at gas mark 3/325°F/170°C. Open packages, marinate with juices and turn; marinate again. Cook a further half hour or until chicken is tender.

# Chiles en Nogada

## Green Peppers in Walnut Sauce

This traditional dish calls for green walnuts which give a truly unique flavour. Green walnuts are ready in September, coinciding with *El Dieciséis de Septiembre,* Mexican Independence Day, when patriotic festivities mark the first uprising against the Spanish in 1810. The colours of the dish are those of the Mexican flag – green, white and red.

---

*2 oz/60 g/²⁄₃ cup ground green walnuts*
*(or blanched almonds and walnuts)*
*6 oz/170 g/¾ cup cream cheese*
*2-4 tbsp milk*
*salt and pepper*
*4 green bell peppers*
Picadillo *made with 8 oz/225 g pork (see p 20), warmed*
*1 small lettuce, shredded*
*8 strips red pepper and/or pomegranate seeds for decoration*

---

Make a masking sauce by mixing the nuts with the cream cheese and a small amount of milk; season. Chill the sauce well as you want a contrast of the very cold sauce with the hot, spicy stuffed peppers. Grill peppers to remove skin. Cut one quarter of the peppers off lengthwise. Fill the peppers with the Picadillo and arrange on the shredded lettuce on a serving dish. Cover with the sauce and garnish with strips of pepper and/or pomegranate seed. You should be able to see green, white and red, the colours of the Mexican flag.

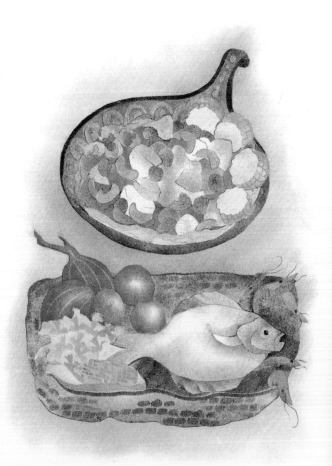

# Seviche

## *Marinated Fish*

Originally from Polynesia, this dish has changed to become authentically Mexican. Marinated fish makes an excellent starter or a luncheon dish on a hot day. It is essential that the fish be absolutely fresh – not frozen.

---

*1 lb/450 g white fish or a mixture of white and shell fish*
*juice 3-4 limes or lemons*
*red onion, thinly sliced*
*large tomato, peeled, seeded and chopped*
*green chilli, chopped*
*2 tbsp fresh coriander or parsley*
*2 fl oz/50 ml/¼ cup corn or olive oil*
*dash Tabasco*
*1 tsp Worcestershire sauce*
*small lettuce, shredded*
*1 corn cob, cooked, cooled and cut into 4 pieces*

---

Skin and cut the fish into 1 in/2½ cm pieces. Put into a glass bowl and pour the juice over it. Make sure the fish is completely covered as it will cook in the juice. Cover and refrigerate at least 8 hours, stirring occasionally. Drain the fish, reserving the juice. Add the onion, tomato, chilli, and coriander to the fish and mix. Make a vinaigrette with the oil and 2 tbsp of the reserved juice, adding the Tabasco and Worcestershire sauces. Pour over the fish and mix. Serve on a bed of lettuce on individual plates. Garnish with corn.

# Huachinango Veracruzano

### *Red Snapper Veracruz-style*

With thousands of miles of coastline, Mexico is a wonderful place to eat fish. The variety is infinite, both of fish and shellfish. Red snapper is usually used in this dish, but if it is not available, use any firm-fleshed white fish.

---

*½ medium onion, finely chopped*
*2 cloves garlic, crushed*
*2 fl oz/50 ml/¼ cup corn oil*
*2 large tomatoes, peeled, seeded and chopped*
*green chilli, finely chopped*
*¼ tsp ground cinnamon*
*½ tsp ground cloves*
*I tsp sugar*
*bay leaf*
*juice of lemon*
*2 tbsp capers, drained*
*4 large red snapper (or cod) fillets, approx I ½ lb/675 g*
*lime quarters*
*stuffed green olives, cut in half*

---

Fry onion and garlic in oil until clear. Add tomatoes, chilli, spices, sugar, and bay leaf and cook 5 minutes. Add lemon juice and capers. Mix well. Put fish in a flat ovenproof dish and cover with the sauce. Bake in a pre-heated oven at gas mark 4/350°F/180°C for 25-30 minutes or until fish is cooked. Garnish with lime quarters and olives. Serve with new potatoes.

# Chayotes Rellenos

## Stuffed Squash

Also known as *choko* or *chow chow*, the chayote is a member of the squash family and botanically is a fruit. It is widely used as a vegetable in south western United States, the West Indies, Australia, and South America. Try West Indian markets for availability.

---

2 chayote, cooked
2 tbsp onion, finely chopped
I egg, beaten
2 oz/60 g/½ cup white cheese, grated
¼ tsp salt
cayenne pepper

---

Cut cooked chayote in half, lengthwise. Remove seeds and scoop pulp from skins. Purée the flesh and mix with onion, egg, cheese and salt. Heap into chayote skins and sprinkle with cayenne pepper. Bake in a pre-heated oven at gas mark 4/350°F/180°C for 20 minutes or until set. By changing the filling to a mixture of beaten eggs, raisins, sugar, sherry, and crumbled sponge cake and baking in the same way until the eggs are set, this becomes an unusual dessert.

# Calabacitas con Elote

## *Courgettes with Corn*

*Calabacitas* (marrows) are one of the staples in the Mexican kitchen – two others are *elote* (corn) and chillis. This dish is best prepared with fresh corn on the cob. If it is the wrong season, use frozen corn kernels.

---

*1 medium onion, roughly chopped*
*1 green chilli*
*2 tbsp corn oil*
*2 large tomatoes, peeled, seeded and chopped*
*½ green pepper, roughly chopped*
*½ red pepper, roughly chopped*
*2 corn cobs cut into quarters or*
*4 oz/125 g/1 cup frozen corn kernels*
*1 lb/450 g courgettes cut into 1 in/2½ cm slices*
*4 oz/125 g/1 cup white cheese, grated*

---

Fry onion and chilli in the oil until soft. Add the tomatoes and peppers and cook 3-4 minutes. Add corn, if fresh, and courgettes. Cover and cook a further 5 minutes. Add corn, if frozen, and cook until vegetables are *al dente*. Stir in cheese and serve.

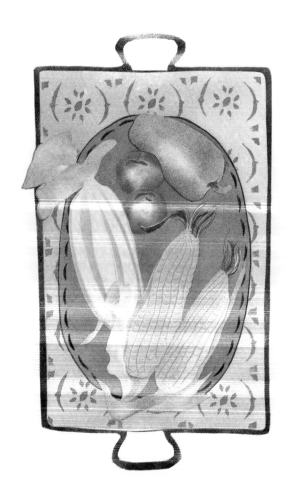

# Ensalada de Nochebuena

*Christmas Eve Salad*

This salad is a traditional dinner dish on 24th December. If time permits, slice the fruit and beetroot and arrange in a circle to represent the full moon. Otherwise, chop and prepare as for a mixed salad.

---

*3 medium beetroot, cooked and peeled*
*2 tart green apples, cored*
*2 bananas*
*2 oranges, peeled and divided into sections*
*4 slices fresh pineapple*
*I small lettuce, shredded*
*pomegranate seeds*
*I tbsp pine kernels*
*¼ pt/150 ml/½ cup corn oil*
*4-5 tbsp lime juice*
*I tsp honey*
*salt and pepper*

---

Prepare the beetroot, fruit and lettuce and arrange the salad as time permits. Reserve the pomegranate seeds and pine kernels as garnish. Make a dressing by combining the corn oil, lime juice, honey, and seasoning. Dress and garnish the salad when ready to serve.

# Fresas con Rompope

## *Strawberries in Rum Punch*

Strawberries or any soft fruit make this an easy, cool dish to finish off a meal which has been especially spicy.

---

*3 punnets strawberries, hulled and cleaned*
*12 oz/350 g/1½ cups caster sugar*
*8 fl oz/225 ml/1 cup double cream*
*5 tbsp Rompope (see p 56)*

---

Reserve 4 of the cleaned strawberries as garnish. Sprinkle the remainder with half the sugar. Set aside and keep cool. Beat the cream with the remaining sugar until stiff. Add the Rompope and mix; it will be thick but runny. This can be done several hours ahead and kept cold. When ready to serve, divide the strawberries among four plates and pour the Rompope mixture over them. Garnish with reserved strawberries.

# Postre de mango

## *Mango Dessert*

Markets in Mexico abound with fresh fruit which can be served as dessert. The variety is such that it is possible to go 2-3 weeks without duplicating the type of fruit served. Made-up desserts take second place to fresh fruit. This dessert is best made not too sweet. This allows the natural flavour of the mango to come through.

---

*1 tbsp gelatine*
*2 tbsp warm water*
*12 fl oz/350 ml/1½ cups mango puréed*
*8 fl oz/225 ml/1 cup double cream*
*2 fl oz/50 ml/¼ cup soured cream*
*2 fl oz/50 ml/¼ cup fresh lime juice*
*honey to taste*

---

Gently dissolve gelatine in warm water. Purée the mango flesh. Add the cream, soured cream, lime juice and gelatine to the mangoes. Process or blend. Add the honey to desired sweetness. Pour into serving bowl and chill. Serve garnished with thin slices of lime and mango.

# Polvorones Naranja

## *Orange Cookies*

These very 'short' biscuits would traditionally have been made with lard. They are delicious prepared that way, but are more healthy made with a combination of butter and margarine.

---

*6 oz/170 g/¾ cup butter and margarine combined*
*2 oz/60 g/½ cup icing sugar*
*grated rind 1 orange*
*2 egg yolks*
*juice 1 orange*
*10 oz/275 g/2½ cups plain flour*
*½ tsp bicarbonate of soda*

---

Cream the fat, icing sugar and grated orange rind until light and fluffy. Beat in the egg yolks and orange juice. Sieve together the flour and soda and add to the butter mixture. Work together until well mixed. Form into a ball and refrigerate at least 2 hours. Roll dough into 1 in/2½ cm balls and place on ungreased baking sheets. Bake in a pre-heated oven at gas mark 6/400°F/200°C for 8-10 minutes until lightly browned. Remove from oven and allow to cool 5 minutes. Roll the cookies in the icing sugar and keep in an airtight container up to a week. The finished cookies may be frozen but without the icing sugar.

# Cacahuete Calientes

## Spicy-hot Peanuts

I was first served these peanuts in a convent-turned-hotel in Oaxaca. They are especially tasty with icy cold beer or with tequila drinks (see p 59). Adjust the hotness by reducing the garlic and peppers. Small dried chiles are available and are a good substitute for *piquin* chillis if you cannot find them.

---

6-8 cloves garlic, whole
I tbsp fresh piquin or small dried chillis
4 tbsp corn oil
8 oz/225 g/2 cups whole raw peanuts
sea salt
lime quarters

---

Cook the garlic and chillis in the oil until the garlic is light gold. Add the peanuts and continue to cook until the peanuts are roasted. Remove with slotted spoon to kitchen paper. Sprinkle with ground sea salt. The peanuts are served warm with wedges of lime to squeeze over them. Other varieties of nuts such as cashews, pistachios, almonds, and so on can be prepared in the same way.

# Rompope

## *Rum Punch*

Rum is a popular drink in Mexico. This rum mixture is a very versatile drink which can be kept in the refrigerator. Drink as is; make a lot of it and serve from a punch bowl sprinkled with cinnamon on a festive occasion; or use as part of a dessert (see p 48).

---

1¾ pt/900 ml/3½ cups whole milk
8 oz/225 g/1 cup sugar
1 cinnamon stick
6 egg yolks
¾ pt/350 ml/1½ cups white rum

---

Combine milk, sugar and cinnamon stick and bring to boil. Cover and simmer for 20 minutes. Remove from heat and cool. Beat egg yolks until thick. Remove cinnamon stick from milk and beat in egg yolks. Return to low heat and allow mixture to thicken. Cool. Mix in rum and decant into a sterilized bottle. Keep refrigerated at least 5 days before using.

# Tequila Drinks

Tequila is a spirit distilled from the maguey plant. It has a very distinctive flavour and can be drunk 'neat' after a lick of salt from a pile on your hand and the juice of half a lime. This is recommended only for the hardy or foolhardy, as the case may be. Golden tequila is often sold with the maguey worm in it.

## Tequila Sunrise

*2 parts tequila*
*4 parts orange juice*
*1 part grenadine syrup*

Mix tequila with the juice. Pour over ice into a tall glass and drizzle grenadine syrup over the top.

## Margarita

*fresh lime, halved*
*salt*
*2 parts tequila*
*1 part orange-flavoured liqueur*
*1 part fresh lime juice*

Rub the rim of a glass with lime half and dip in salt, shaking off any excess. The glass may be frozen at this point. Combine tequila, liqueur and lime juice in an ice-filled shaker and strain into glass. Both of these drinks can be successfully prepared in large quantities.

# Index